The Grosset & Dunlap
Read Aloud Library

This book belongs to

The Grosset & Dunlap Read Aloud Library

BIBLE STORIES
From the Old Testament

BIBLE

Publishers • GROSSET & DUNLAP • New York

STORIES
From the Old Testament

Retold by Linda Hayward
Illustrated by Katherine Dietz Coville

A member of The Putnam Publishing Group

To my mother and father,
who launched me down the road less traveled.
K.D.C.

Copyright © 1987 by Linda Hayward.
Illustrations copyright © 1987 by Katherine Dietz Coville.
All rights reserved.
Published by Grosset & Dunlap, a member of The Putnam Publishing Group, New York.
Published simultaneously in Canada.
Printed and bound in Singapore.
Library of Congress Catalog Card Number: 86-83306
ISBN 0-448-10351-6   A B C D E F G H I J

CONTENTS

THE BEGINNING

Before there were living creatures on the earth, before there were birds flying in the sky, before there were fish swimming in the sea, before there was a sun, before there was a moon, before heaven or earth itself, there was God.

And God said, "Let there be light."

And there was light.

And God saw that it was good.

And God said, "Let there be heaven, let there be earth; let there be a sun and a moon; let there be oceans, and fish to swim in them; let there be sky, and birds to fly in it; let there be land, and let the land be filled with creatures of every kind."

God created all these things.

And God saw that it was good.

And God said, "Let there be two who will take care of the earth and be masters of all the creatures."

So God created man and woman. He created them in His own image.

And God saw everything that He had made, and it was very good.

GENESIS

THE GARDEN OF EDEN

The first man and woman were named Adam and Eve, and they lived in a beautiful garden that God made for them. The garden was in a place on earth called Eden.

The Garden of Eden was full of trees and vines, flowers and ferns. Through the garden there flowed a stream of cool, bubbling water. God placed many creatures in the garden to keep Adam and Eve company: the frog and the turtle, the stork and the dove, the bee and the butterfly, the lion and the lamb.

In the middle of the garden God planted a special tree. He called it the Tree of Knowledge of Good and Evil.

"You may eat the fruit that grows on any tree in the garden," God said to Adam and Eve. "But you must not eat the fruit that grows on the Tree of Knowledge."

Adam and Eve promised to obey God and not to eat the forbidden fruit.

In the garden there also lived a serpent, who was the slyest of creatures. One day the serpent saw Eve standing under the Tree of Knowledge and spoke to her.

"Did God say that you could eat the fruit that grows on any tree in the garden?" the serpent asked.

"He told us that we could eat any fruit," said Eve, "except the fruit that grows on this tree, the Tree of Knowledge."

"But the fruit on this tree looks the most delicious of all," said the serpent.

Eve looked up at the plump, juicy fruit dangling from the branches of the tree, and she saw that this was true.

"The fruit that grows on the Tree of Knowledge will make you wise," said the serpent. "God told you not to eat it because he did not want you and Adam to know what He knows."

Eve thought: *Surely it would be wonderful to know what God knows.*

Eve reached up and plucked a piece of fruit and tasted it. Then she went to Adam and told him what the serpent had said, and he took a bite of the fruit, too.

Then Adam and Eve looked at each other, and for the first time they were ashamed of their nakedness.

In the evening, when they heard God walking in the garden, they were frightened and hid from Him.

"Adam. Eve," called God. "Where are you?"

"We are here," said Adam. "We heard you coming, and we were ashamed."

"Why are you ashamed?" asked God. "Did you eat the fruit that grows on the Tree of Knowledge?"

Adam and Eve told God that the serpent had tempted them and that they did eat the fruit.

And God was angry. He was angry with the serpent and punished him, saying to the serpent that he would have to crawl on his belly in the dust all of his days.

God was angry with Adam and Eve, too, because they had disobeyed Him.

"Now that you have eaten the fruit that grows on the Tree of Knowledge," God said to them, "you will know both good and evil. You will know happiness, but you will also know sadness. With wisdom comes sorrow."

And God sent Adam and Eve out of the Garden of Eden.

But after they had gone into the world, God continued to watch over them.

GENESIS

13

CAIN AND ABEL

Adam and Eve had two sons named Cain and Abel. The two brothers grew into strong young men, but it happened that one brother pleased God and one did not.

Abel was a keeper of sheep, and when he gave God a gift, it was the finest lamb in his flock. Cain worked the fields and was a planter of seeds, but his gifts to God were not the finest that he could give.

When Cain saw that God liked Abel's present but not his own, he was angry.

And God said to Cain, "Why are you angry? If you do well, you will know that I love you."

But Cain did not understand God, and his anger grew. Finally Cain said to Abel, "Let us go into the fields by ourselves." When the two brothers were alone, Cain killed Abel.

Cain was by himself, and God spoke to him and said, "Where is your brother Abel?"

"I don't know," said Cain. "Am I my brother's keeper?"

But God knew what Cain had done.

And God punished him, saying, "Cain, you will never again dig or plant seed and watch it grow. The earth will give you nothing. You must wander from place to place, looking for food."

And Cain went away into a strange land.

GENESIS

NOAH'S ARK

Long after the days of Adam and Eve, there were many people on the earth. Most of the people did not pray to God. Evil was everywhere. There was fighting and stealing and killing. God was sorry that He had made the world.

There came a time when only one man still listened to God, and his name was Noah. Noah was a good man, and he tried to do what God wanted him to do.

God decided at last to destroy everything on earth, but He wanted to save Noah and his family.

"Build an ark," God said to Noah. "Build it out of wood and seal it with pitch. Build it three stories high, with a roof over the top and a door in the side. And when the ark is built and stocked with food, go into it with your wife and children. And bring animals onto the ark. Bring on two of every kind, male and female."

Noah did not question God's strange commands. He did exactly what God told him to do. He built an ark out of wood and sealed it with pitch. He made it three stories high, with a roof over the top and a door in the side. And when the ark was finished and stocked with food, Noah went into it with his wife. His sons and his sons' wives and children went in, too.

Then through the big door in the side of the ark went all the animals, two by two. In went the lion and the lioness, the buck and the doe, the bull and the cow, the ram and the ewe. No beast was too big. No insect was too small. In went the elephants. In went the ants.

Then God closed the door.

And God opened the heavens.

It began to rain.
It rained for forty
days and forty nights.
It rained so hard that
the water covered the
land. It flooded the
fields, it flooded the
houses. It covered the trees, it
covered the mountaintops, too.

And every living thing on the earth was drowned in God's great flood.

But Noah's ark floated on top of the water. Noah and his family and the animals inside the ark were saved.

Then God closed the heavens, and He sent a wind to dry up the water.

Inside the ark Noah waited. Days turned into weeks, weeks turned into months, and still Noah waited. But Noah did not think that God had forgotten him. He trusted God.

One year after Noah first went into the ark, God spoke to him and told him to come out. And Noah did. He and his wife and his sons and their wives and children walked out of the ark onto the dry land.

And right behind Noah came the animals. Out they came, two by two. Out came the tigers, out came the camels;

out came the bears and the ostriches, too. Some came crawling, some came walking; some came hopping, some flying. But out they all came, two by two.

And Noah felt his feet touch the earth once more. He fell down on his knees and thanked God for keeping him safe.

Noah's prayer pleased God. And because of Noah, God made the first rainbow. He put His bow of colors in the sky as a promise to Noah, and to all those who would come after Noah, that He would never again send a flood to destroy the earth.

GENESIS

THE TOWER OF BABEL

Long after the time of Noah there were again many people in the land, and they decided to build a city for themselves.

"Come, let us make bricks," said the people, and so they did. They formed bricks out of clay and baked them in the sun, and when they saw what they could do, the people were pleased with themselves.

"Now, let us build houses," said the people, and so they did. They put bricks together with mortar and made houses and all the other buildings they needed for their city. And when the people saw what they had built, they were even more pleased with themselves.

It was not long before someone thought of building a tower, a tower so tall that it would go all the way to heaven.

Down went the bricks, up went the tower. Up and up and up until it was very high indeed.

Then God frowned because the people thought they could get to heaven without His help. God decided to teach the people a lesson. He changed the one language that they spoke into many languages. Suddenly the people who had been working on the great tower could not understand each other, and so they could no longer work together.

The people listened to each other babbling and were frightened. Off they went in every direction across the land.

GENESIS

THE PROMISED LAND

In a place known as Haran, there lived a wise man named Abraham. Abraham was descended from Noah. Like Noah, he believed in one great God, creator of all things. Abraham was surrounded by people who did not believe in one God. Some worshipped many gods. Some worshipped none at all.

God saw that Abraham loved Him above all others, and He spoke to Abraham. "Leave this place," God said. "Leave your home and this country. Follow me, and I will show you a new land. I will bless you and make you the father of a great nation."

Abraham and his wife, Sarah, gathered their servants and their belongings and set out on the mysterious journey. They followed God, and He led them to a new land, the land of Canaan. It was a good land, and they settled down there to live.

Years passed, and Abraham grew rich and powerful. He had many sheep and cattle, and his wisdom increased. Everyone around Abraham looked up to him. He and Sarah had almost everything they could have wished for. But they did not have children, which God had promised to them.

One day, when Abraham was an old man, he sat outside his tent and saw three men standing in front of him. Suddenly he knew that these were not ordinary men. They were sent by God.

Abraham called to Sarah, and she brought water to the thirsty visitors. Abraham urged them to rest under a shady tree. Sarah told her servants to prepare the finest meal possible.

After the meal, one of the strangers told Abraham that God would make it possible for Sarah to give birth to a son the next year.

Sarah laughed when she heard what the stranger had said. And the stranger asked, "Why do you laugh, Sarah?"

"Because I am too old to have a child," said Sarah.

"There is nothing God cannot do," the man said.

Then Sarah felt the power of God, and she was afraid.

"Do not be afraid," said the stranger. "God has promised it."

And Sarah gave birth to a son in the following year and named him Isaac, and she thanked God for the child.

When Isaac was grown, he had many children. His children had children, and by and by there were a great many people who were the descendants of Abraham and Sarah. The land of Canaan was their land, as God had promised, and Abraham was the father of a great nation.

GENESIS

THE WICKED CITY

In the time of Abraham, there was a city so wicked that God decided to destroy it. The city was called Sodom, and it was full of thieves and murderers. But there was a good man named Lot who lived in the city. He was the nephew of Abraham.

God wanted to save Lot's life, and so He sent two angels at night into the city. The angels said to Lot, "You must leave the city, for God is about to destroy this evil place."

Lot did not want to leave his home, but early the next morning he led his wife and two daughters out of their house and out of Sodom. When they were on the road away from the city, they stopped to rest.

"You must not stop!" said the angels. "Run to the far hills, and no matter what happens, do not look back."

Then the earth around the great city of Sodom began to tremble. The sky above was full of fire, and red-hot stones fell down on the houses. Everything within the city walls was burned to ashes.

Lot and his family were safe on the road beyond the city. But when they felt the fire behind them, Lot's wife forgot the angels' warning and looked back. Instantly she was turned into a pillar of salt. Lot and his daughters wept, even as they thanked God for sparing their lives.

GENESIS

REBEKAH AT THE WELL

Abraham's beloved child Isaac grew up in the land of Canaan and was a good son to his aging father. Then it was time for Isaac to marry. Abraham wanted his son to marry a woman who believed in one great God as he and his family did.

To find such a woman, and because he was too old to travel, Abraham asked his most trusted servant to journey out of Canaan and go to the country where Abraham's relatives lived. There the servant was to find a wife for Isaac and bring her back.

But the servant did not think he would know which woman was the right one for Isaac.

"How will I do this?" the servant asked.

"With God's help," said Abraham. "His angel will guide you."

The servant prepared for his journey. He took ten camels laden with gifts for the bride and began his travels to the far place.

At last the servant came to the town where Abraham's relatives lived. He stopped at the well outside the town. It was early evening, and young women from the town were coming to fill their water jars.

The servant still feared that he would not know which woman to choose, and so he asked God to help him.

"Lord, let there be a sign so I will know what to do," said the servant. "I will ask one of the women for a drink of water. If she is to be the wife of Isaac, let her say, 'Drink, and I will get water for your camels, too.'"

As the servant finished his prayer, a pretty young woman came up to the well. Abraham's servant went to her and said, "Would you give me a drink of water?"

The young woman looked at the tired traveler and answered, "Please, drink, and I will get water for your camels, too."

When the servant heard her words, he was glad. He asked the young woman her name. It was Rebekah, and her family was related to the family of Abraham, the servant's master.

The servant thanked God silently, for surely this was the woman who was meant to be the wife of Isaac.

And the next day, Rebekah left her home and her family and went with the servant to the land of Canaan. She rode on a camel. As they neared the place where Isaac lived, Rebekah saw a young man coming toward her. His eyes met hers, and she could not look away.

"Who is the man who comes?" asked Rebekah.

"He is Isaac," replied the servant.

Then Rebekah felt shy, and she pulled her veil over her face. Isaac came and took her hand, and they were married.

GENESIS

JACOB AND ESAU

Isaac, the son of Abraham, was blessed by God and became wise and powerful and also wealthy.

When Isaac's wife, Rebekah, was about to have her first child, God spoke to her. "You will have two sons," God said. "And the second-born son shall one day inherit his father's blessing."

Rebekah gave birth to twin boys, and their names were Esau and Jacob. Esau was the first-born.

When the sons were grown and Isaac was an old man, the father called for Esau, his first-born son, to give him his blessing and make Esau the leader of the family.

But Rebekah remembered that God had said that Jacob, the second-born, would inherit his father's blessing.

Rebekah told Jacob to dress himself in Esau's clothing and to go to his father and pretend to be Esau.

Jacob did what his mother told him to do.

"Here I am, Father," said Jacob. "I am Esau."

Isaac could not see well and believed that the young man was his first-born. And so he gave his blessing and his lands and wealth to Jacob instead of Esau.

When Esau found out that his brother had stolen his blessing, Esau was angry and said he would kill Jacob.

Jacob's mother told him to go away and live with his uncle in a distant land until his brother was ready to forgive him.

Jacob started off on his long journey, but he felt frightened and troubled. He did not know if what he had done was right.

One night during his travels, when Jacob could find no shelter, he lay down on the ground to sleep. And that night he had a dream.

Jacob dreamed that he saw a ladder going up to heaven. Angels were climbing up and down the ladder. And God spoke to Jacob and said, "I am the God of Abraham. I am the God of your father, Isaac. And the land on which you lie, I give to you and your descendants."

Then Jacob woke up. "The Lord is with me," he said. "And I did not know it."

Jacob lived with his uncle for many years and never forgot God's words or the ladder that went up to heaven.

At last God told Jacob to go back to his father's house, where his brother Esau still lived. Jacob was afraid that his brother would still be angry with him, but he prepared for the journey home.

When Jacob came to the place where he had lived as a child, he saw his brother Esau running toward him. Esau put his arms around Jacob and kissed him. Then both brothers wept because they had been apart for so long. And Esau forgave Jacob for taking the blessing of their father, Isaac.

GENESIS

Joseph and His Brothers

Jacob had twelve sons. His favorite was a gentle boy named Joseph. Joseph had ten older brothers and one who was younger.

Because Jacob loved Joseph, he gave his son a special coat to wear, a coat of many colors. When the older brothers saw Joseph wearing his new coat, they were jealous.

One night, Joseph had a dream. He dreamed that he was powerful and that his brothers bowed down to him. When he told his brothers about the dream, they hated him.

Jacob, the father of Joseph, was a wealthy man with many sheep and goats and acres of land. His oldest sons looked after the flocks, but Joseph and his younger brother stayed at home with their father. One day Joseph went out to the fields to see his brothers.

When the brothers saw him coming, they decided to kill him. They grabbed Joseph and tore off his beautiful coat. They found a deep pit and threw him into it. Then they went away and left him to die. When they got home, they told their father that Joseph had been killed by wild animals.

But Joseph did not die. A group of merchants bound for Egypt came by and saw Joseph and pulled him out of the pit. They took him out of the land of Canaan to Egypt, where they sold him to a rich man.

But Joseph loved God and was loved by God in return, and no harm could come to him.

Joseph was a slave, and one day he was accused of a crime, one that he did not commit. He was taken to prison and thrown into a dungeon.

Two other men happened to be put in prison with Joseph. These two had worked in the palace of the Pharaoh, or king. One was a butler, and one was a baker.

One night the butler and the baker each had a dream. In the morning they wondered what their dreams could mean.

"Tell me what you dreamt," said Joseph.

And so they did. The butler said that in his dream he crushed grapes, and the juice filled Pharaoh's cup. And Joseph said to the butler, "Your dream means that you will soon be let out of prison."

The baker, on the other hand, told Joseph that he had seen birds in his dream that were eating the royal bread baked for Pharaoh. And Joseph said sadly, "Your dream means that you will soon be sentenced to die."

Three days later Joseph's words came true. The poor baker was hanged. The butler was freed from prison and was sent back to the palace to work for Pharaoh.

Joseph stayed in his dungeon and was forgotten by everyone—everyone, that is, except Pharaoh's butler. The butler knew that Joseph had a gift from God that allowed him to see into the future.

One night Pharaoh had a dream, a dream so strange that he called for all the magicians and wise men in Egypt to come and tell him what it meant. But no one understood Pharaoh's dream.

Then the palace butler told Pharaoh about a young man in prison who understood dreams. Pharaoh told the guards to bring this man to him.

When Joseph appeared, Pharaoh said, "They tell me that you understand dreams."

And Joseph answered, "Not I, but God."

Then Pharaoh told Joseph his dream. "I was standing on the banks of the river Nile," he said. "Seven fat, healthy cows came out of the water. After them came seven cows who were thin and hungry. Then the thin cows ate up the fat cows."

And Joseph said to Pharaoh, "In your dream, God is telling you what He is going to do. The seven fat cows stand for seven years of good harvest, when there will be food for everyone. The seven thin cows mean seven years of bad harvest when there will not be enough food."

Joseph told Pharaoh that the farmers in Egypt should store food and grain during the good years so that the people would have enough to eat in the bad years.

Pharaoh listened and saw that Joseph was wise. He made Joseph the governor of Egypt and told him to make sure that food was saved in the years to come.

Everything happened just as Joseph had said. First came seven good years. During this time, Joseph saw that food was stored away. Then came seven bad years when nothing would grow. The people cried out for food.

And Pharaoh said, "Go and see Joseph."

And Joseph took food from the storehouses and gave it to the people.

In the lands beyond Egypt, people were also hungry. In the land of Canaan, where Joseph had lived, there was not enough to eat. Joseph's father, Jacob, sent his sons on the long journey down to Egypt to buy food.

Joseph's brothers went to Egypt and came before Pharaoh's powerful governor. And the dream Joseph had had many years before came true. His brothers came before him and bowed down to him.

Joseph recognized the men and knew they were his brothers. But they did not know that the governor was, in fact, Joseph. They did not recognize their brother in his fine Egyptian robes.

"I am Joseph," he said to them, "the one that you left in a pit to die."

When his brothers heard this, they cried out and were ashamed. But Joseph forgave them and gave them food. Then he brought all the family of Jacob, his father, to Egypt. He cared for many people who came from the land of Canaan because it was the will of God.

GENESIS

MOSES IN THE BULRUSHES

The people of Canaan who went down to Egypt lived in that land for many years. Jacob, the son of Isaac and father of Joseph, lived in Egypt, too. Before he died, God blessed Jacob and called him Israel. The many sons, and grandsons, and great-grandchildren of Jacob grew to be known as the Israelites, or the children of Israel.

The Israelites followed the laws of God. Therefore, they could not always obey the laws of Pharaoh, the king of Egypt. Pharaoh grew very angry and decided to punish the Israelites. He told his guards to find all the newborn sons of these people and to throw them in the Nile River.

Many babies were taken away, and the Israelite women wept. But one mother thought of a way to save her baby son. She made a cradle out of the bulrushes that grew along the river bank and put her baby in it. She set the cradle among the reeds of the river near Pharaoh's palace.

That day Pharaoh's daughter came down to the Nile to bathe as usual. She saw the cradle floating among the tall grasses and told a maid to fetch it. When she saw the baby inside the cradle, she knew that he was a child of the Israelites. But Pharaoh's daughter felt tenderness toward the baby and wanted him to live. And the boy grew up in Pharaoh's palace. His name was Moses, and he was loved by God.

EXODUS

THE BURNING BUSH

The Israelites who lived in Egypt became slaves to Pharaoh. Their lives were hard and without joy.

Moses, who grew up in the palace of the Pharaoh, was also an Israelite. He saw the sorrowful life of his people and left Egypt and went to live in a distant land.

Moses became a shepherd. One day he led his flocks to the side of a mountain, and there he saw a strange thing happening. He saw a bush that was growing on the mountainside catch fire. He watched the fire and saw that the bush was not burning. He went closer.

Then a voice called to him from the fire: "Moses. Moses."

And Moses answered, "I am here."

The voice said, "I am the God of your forefathers, the God of Abraham and of Isaac and of Jacob." And Moses covered his face because he was afraid to look at God.

Then God said, "I have heard the cry of my people in Egypt. I have seen their misery. I have come down to save them and to take them to a land that is flowing with milk and honey. Come now, and go to Pharaoh, for you will be the one to lead the children of Israel out of Egypt."

And Moses was frightened. He did not think he would be able to do what the Lord wanted. So God sent Moses' brother Aaron to help him. And God promised to guide Moses and Aaron, and to be with them always.

EXODUS

THE PLAGUES

Moses and his brother Aaron went back to the land of Egypt, as God had told them to do. They gathered together the Israelites, or Hebrews, who were slaves in that land.

Moses told the Hebrews that God wanted them to be free and to leave Egypt and to go to a new land.

Then the Hebrews knew that God had heard their cries and had sent Moses to them, and they were filled with hope.

Moses and Aaron went to the palace of the Pharaoh and told him that God wanted the Hebrew slaves to be free to leave Egypt.

But Pharaoh did not believe in the God of the Hebrews. He laughed at Moses and said, "Who is this God that I, Pharaoh, should obey Him? I will not let Israel go."

Moses took the staff that God had given him and threw it on the ground. The staff became a snake, and everyone was amazed. When Moses took hold of the snake by its tail, it changed back into a rod.

Still Pharaoh would not agree to let the Hebrews go.

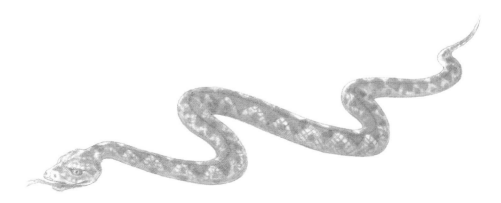

Then Moses held his staff over the Nile River, as God told him to do, and the water turned to blood. The fish died, and there was nothing to drink. But Pharaoh told the people to dig wells, and they did. They found clean water, and Pharaoh did not let the Hebrews go.

Pharaoh would not hear the word of God, and so the Lord sent terrible plagues to Egypt, one after another.

First He sent thousands of frogs to plague the people. The frogs hopped out of the Nile River and filled the houses of the Egyptians. But there were no frogs in the houses of the Hebrews.

God filled the air
with great swarms of
flies and other insects.
He sent a disease that
killed the cattle and the
sheep. He created a wind
and sent hailstones that swept
over the land and destroyed the crops.
Locusts came, and there was not a leaf left on any
tree. Then God sent darkness, and for three days
the Egyptians lived without light.

But in the places where the Hebrews lived, none of
these things happened.

And each time there was a plague, Pharaoh agreed to let
the Hebrew people go. But when the plague was over,
Pharaoh broke his promise and would not allow the Hebrews
to leave Egypt.

At last Moses said to Pharaoh, "Hear the word of the
Lord. You are to humble yourself before Him and let His
people leave this land. If you do not, He will bring upon
you one last plague, worse than all the others."

But Pharaoh was stubborn and would not listen.

EXODUS

53

THE NIGHT OF THE PASSOVER

od told Moses that when He brought the final plague
to Egypt, Pharaoh would agree at last to let the Israelites go.

Moses told the Hebrews what God had said. And he
told them to kill a lamb and to dip herbs in the blood of the
lamb. They were to sprinkle the blood on the doorway of
each Hebrew house.

"The Lord will go through Egypt and punish every
family," said Moses, "but when He sees the blood of a lamb
on a doorway, He will pass over that door and will not
allow death to come into that house. And after all this has
happened, Pharaoh will set us free.

"And when you have entered the land which God will give you," Moses said, "you shall keep this day in remembrance, from generation to generation."

The Israelites went and did what the Lord had asked.

That night there was a great cry in Egypt, for in every Egyptian house the first-born child was dead. In the homes of the Hebrews, no one died. Pharaoh's oldest son was dead, too, and Pharaoh begged Moses and Aaron to take the Hebrews out of the land before there were more deaths.

When it was still night, the Israelites took their bread dough before it had risen, gathered their belongings, and followed Moses and Aaron out of Egypt. And God showed them the way.

EXODUS

CROSSING THE RED SEA

Thousands of Israelites, with herds of sheep and cattle, followed Moses out of Egypt. God moved before them as a great cloud by day and a pillar of fire by night.

When they reached the edge of the Red Sea, the Israelites made camp. It was then that they heard the sound of horses and chariots behind them. Pharaoh's army was coming to take them back to Egypt. They were trapped between the army and the sea.

But Moses told the people not to be afraid. He held his staff out over the sea, as God told him to do, and God brought a strong wind and made the waters separate. A dry path appeared between two great walls of sea water. The Israelites rushed forward onto the path.

Behind them came the army of Pharaoh. They, too, marched between the walls of water.

At last the Israelites reached the far shore. Then God let the watery walls fall down. The sea fell on the army of Pharaoh, and every soldier was drowned.

When the children of Israel saw the power of God, they gave thanks and sang together:

I will sing to the Lord,
for He has risen up in triumph;
the horse and his rider
He has hurled into the sea.

EXODUS

57

Manna from Heaven

Moses led the Israelites from the Red Sea into the wilderness of the desert beyond. For three days they traveled in the heat and found no water. "What are we to drink?" asked the people, and they were angry at Moses and Aaron. And God led them to a cool place where there were palm trees and water wells.

They traveled on, for days and days, and the food supply grew low. "What are we to eat?" asked the people, and again they were angry.

God spoke to Moses, and Moses spoke to the people. "When evening comes," said Moses, "you will know that God is with us. And when morning comes, you will see the glory of the Lord."

In the evening quails flew all around the camp.

In the morning fine white flakes covered the ground. It was food sent by God, and the Israelites called it manna. They made little cakes, and the cakes tasted of honey.

There was manna for the people each morning when they awoke. On the sixth morning, Moses said, "Tomorrow is the day of rest, the Lord's sabbath. Prepare enough food today for two days. For tomorrow you will find no manna in the field."

And the Lord gave this food to the Israelites for the whole of the long journey to Canaan.

EXODUS

THE TEN COMMANDMENTS

Three months after the Hebrews left Egypt, they came to Mount Sinai, the mountain of God. They put up their tents and camped there.

Early one morning Moses gathered the people at the bottom of the mountain. It was the day when the Lord was to come down on Mount Sinai. There was thunder and lightning in the air, and a thick cloud lay on the mountain.

Then the mountain was covered with smoke, and the Lord descended on it in fire. The mountain trembled and shook and was like a furnace, and the people were frightened.

God called Moses up to the top of the mountain, and Moses went up. There God gave him ten laws— ten commandments for the people of Israel to live by. The commandments were written down on two tablets of stone.

And these were the commandments of the Lord:

You shall have no other gods before me.
You shall not pray to any carved images.
You shall not use the name of God in any careless way.
Remember the Sabbath and keep it holy.
Honor your father and your mother.
You shall not kill.
You shall not commit adultery.
You shall not steal.
You shall not bring false charges against anyone.
You shall not try to gain what belongs to others.

Moses stayed on the mountaintop for many days, and the people below grew restless and afraid. They began to think that Moses would not return. They began to think that the God of Moses would not help them find their way through the wilderness.

They doubted God, and so they melted their gold jewelry and made a new god out of gold, a golden calf. The people sang and danced around the calf, and they prayed to it.

After forty days Moses came down from the mountain. With him he carried the word of God.

When Moses saw that the people were praying to a golden calf, he was so angry that he threw down the stone tablets, and they broke into pieces.

"You have not trusted God," cried Moses. "God said that you shall not pray to any other god, and you have broken his first commandment."

The people were sorry for the way they had behaved.

Again Moses talked with God on the mountain, and God forgave the people and wrote His commandments on new tablets. When Moses came down from the mountain this time, his face was shining with the light of God. His face shone so brightly that the people were afraid to look at him.

Moses explained the word of God, and the people listened.

EXODUS

THE WALLS OF JERICHO

The Israelites lived in the wilderness for forty years before God let them reach Canaan, the promised land. And before they entered Canaan, their leader, Moses, servant of the Lord, died and was buried by his people.

Then God put a strong, courageous man named Joshua in command of the Israelites. Joshua led the people across the river Jordan and into Canaan. It was a good land where grapevines, figs, and pomegranates grew, a land that flowed with milk and honey.

The people who already lived in that land were afraid of the Israelites. They had heard that the God of Israel had dried up the waters of the Red Sea so that His people might leave Egypt. They had heard that the powerful God of Israel

wanted His people to have a new land, a land they were coming to at last.

One great city in that land, the walled city of Jericho, closed its gates to the Israelites. The people inside were frightened, and no one went out or came in.

Then God told Joshua how he and his people could capture the city. "Each day for six days you and your soldiers shall march around the city," God said. "And there will be seven priests who shall carry trumpets. On the seventh day, you shall march around the city seven times. The seven priests will blow on their trumpets, and all the people will shout one great shout together. And when you do this, the walls of Jericho will fall."

Joshua woke up early on the morning of the first day and led his men around the city as God had told him to do. No one made a sound. And seven priests of God went with them, each carrying a trumpet.

On the second day they went around the city again. And they marched each day for six days.

On the seventh day Joshua woke at dawn and marched his soldiers around the city again, but this time they went around it seven times.

Then the seven priests blew on their trumpets, and it was a wonderful sound.

Then Joshua called out to his army, "Shout! For the Lord has given us the city!"

And the soldiers shouted loudly together, and the thousands of voices became one great voice. And the walls of the city of Jericho all came tumbling down.

JOSHUA

Samuel, Child of God

The Israelites had lived in Canaan for many years, and among them was a Hebrew woman whose name was Hannah. Hannah longed to have children, but she had none. She prayed to God and told Him that if He gave her a son, she would see that the boy did the work of the Lord all his life.

Soon after this, Hannah gave birth to a boy, and she named him Samuel.

When Samuel was still young, Hannah took him to the temple. She asked the priest, whose name was Eli, to look after her son and keep him in God's house.

Eli was old and was glad to have the boy help him to shine the lamps and to light them, and to care for everything in the temple. And Samuel was happy in the house of the Lord.

Eli had two grown sons of his own. His sons did not obey the Lord, and God was angry with them.

One night Samuel was in bed when he heard a voice call, "Samuel." He hopped out of bed and ran to Eli's room, thinking it was Eli who was calling.

"I did not call you," said Eli gently. "Go back to bed."

As soon as the boy was back in bed, the voice called again, saying, "Samuel." Again he ran to Eli's room.

"Here I am," said Samuel.

"But I did not call," said Eli, as before. "Go back to bed."

Once again the voice called out, "Samuel." And once again the boy went to Eli.

This time Eli, the priest, knew that it was God who was calling to Samuel.

"Go back to bed," the priest told the boy. "But if you hear your name again, say *Speak, Lord, your servant hears you.*"

So Samuel went back to his bed. And the voice called, "Samuel. Samuel."

And the boy answered, "Speak, Lord, your servant hears you."

And God spoke to Samuel. He told him that Eli's sons would be punished for their disobedience to God.

In the morning Samuel did not want to talk to Eli. He was afraid to tell the priest what God had said about Eli's sons. Then Eli called Samuel to him, and the boy went.

"Did God talk to you?" asked Eli. "What did He say?"

Samuel told Eli the truth, that his sons were to be punished. And Eli knew it was the will of the Lord.

Not long after this, the Israelites fought a great battle. Eli's sons joined in the battle, and both of them were killed. Then Eli saw that God had chosen Samuel, the boy, to speak for Him. And Samuel was a prophet of the Lord all his days.

I SAMUEL

DAVID AND GOLIATH

In the days of Samuel, the first king of the Israelites was chosen, and his name was Saul. Saul led the people into many battles against their enemies, the Philistines. But Saul disobeyed the laws of the Lord, and God was sorry He had made Saul king.

God chose a future king for the Israelites, a shepherd boy named David, who was the youngest son of Jesse of Bethlehem. Samuel the prophet anointed David with holy oil, and the spirit of the Lord was with David from that day on.

David loved God and played his harp and sang joyful songs to the Lord. One day he was sent to play and sing for King Saul, who was troubled and filled with evil spirits. Saul felt well again after David played his music, and the king asked that David stay with him.

Time passed, and the Israelites were again at war with the Philistines. The armies camped on two hills, and between the hills was a valley. Down from the camp of the Philistines came a giant of a man named Goliath. He was more than nine feet tall. He was armed with a heavy coat of mail and a huge helmet of brass. The staff of his huge spear was like a beam of wood.

Goliath stood and cried out to the armies of Israel, "Send me your strongest man, that he and I may do battle!"

Not one Israelite soldier dared to go down and fight Goliath. Every morning and every evening for forty days, the giant Philistine challenged the Israelites.

And David, son of Jesse, saw Goliath frighten the soldiers of Israel. At last he said, "Who is this man that he should challenge the armies of the living God?"

And David said, "I will go and fight the giant. The Lord who saved me from the lion and the bear who came to kill my sheep will save me from the Philistine."

And David refused to wear the armor of a soldier. He took only the sling he used as a shepherd and five smooth stones, and he went down to where Goliath stood. The men in both armies watched in silence.

When Goliath saw David, he roared with laughter. "What!" he shouted. "Am I a dog to be teased by a boy with stones?"

And David answered, "The battle is the Lord's, and He will give you into the hands of Israel."

As Goliath raised his massive spear, David put one stone in his sling and aimed carefully. The stone flew through the air like an arrow and hit Goliath hard on the forehead. Goliath fell down and lay dead on the earth.

When the Philistines saw that their champion was dead, they fled. And it was a great victory for all of Israel.

I SAMUEL

King David and the Ark of the Covenant

When Saul died, David became the king of the Israelites. He was a good ruler and a powerful general, and he led the armies of Israel to victory again and again.

When there was peace in the land, King David made Jerusalem the center of his kingdom, and it was called the city of David.

The king built a beautiful city, and the people of Israel were proud of it. But most of all, David wanted to build a temple in Jerusalem, a temple to house the Ark of the Covenant, where the tablets of God were kept.

When the Ark was brought into Jerusalem, there was a great procession and much rejoicing. There was singing everywhere, and the sound of lutes and tambourines, castanets and cymbals. King David himself danced with joy before the Lord.

But when David wanted to begin building his great temple for the Ark, God stopped him.

God spoke to a prophet in Jerusalem named Nathan, and He said, "Tell David that I have made him prince over my people Israel. But a child of David's shall one day come after him, and it is he who shall build a house in honor of my name."

David heard the word of God and gave thanks.

II SAMUEL

76

THE PSALMS OF DAVID

In the book of Psalms are the songs of the Israelites. It is thought that some of the most beautiful of these were written by David, son of Jesse.

Psalm 23

The Lord is my shepherd, I shall not want;
He maketh me to lie down in green pastures,
He leadeth me beside the still waters,
He restoreth my soul.
He leadeth me in the paths of righteousness for His name's sake.
Yea, though I walk through the valley of the shadow of death,
I will fear no evil, for thou art with me;
Thy rod and Thy staff, they comfort me.
Thou preparest a table before me in the presence of my enemies;
Thou anointest my head with oil,
My cup runneth over.
Surely goodness and mercy shall follow me
All the days of my life,
And I will dwell in the house of the Lord forever.

Psalm 100

Make a joyful noise unto the Lord, all ye lands;
Serve the Lord with gladness,
Come before His presence with singing,
Know ye that the Lord, He is God.
It is He that hath made us, and not we ourselves;
We are His people, and the sheep of His pasture.
Enter into His gates with thanksgiving,
And into His courts with praise.
Be thankful unto Him, and bless His name,
For the Lord is good, His mercy is everlasting,
And His truth endureth to all generations.

THE WISDOM OF SOLOMON

When King David died, his son Solomon became king of Israel. And God came to Solomon in a dream one night and said, "Solomon, I shall give you anything you wish. What do you ask of me?"

Instead of asking for riches or a long life, as others might have done, Solomon said, "Give me a wise and understanding heart, O Lord, that I may judge your people well."

God was pleased with Solomon's request and gave him more wisdom than any man on earth.

Many people brought their troubles before the king, for Solomon's wisdom made him a good and fair judge. One day two women appeared before Solomon. One was carrying a baby. Each woman said that the baby belonged to her.

One pointed to the other and said, "We live in the same house, and her baby died in the night. While I was sleeping, she came and took my baby. She put her dead child in my baby's place."

"That is a lie!" cried the other. "Her baby died, and now she wants mine."

While the women argued, King Solomon called for his sword. "Each of you claims the child is yours," he said. "Therefore I will divide the child in half."

"It is the only fair thing," said the first woman.

But the second woman cried out, "No! Give the baby to her if you must, only do not hurt him."

Then King Solomon declared that the baby belonged to the second woman. "She is the real mother," he said. "A true mother would rather give up her child than see him killed."

When the people of Israel heard the king's judgment, they knew that Solomon had the wisdom of God within him. People of all lands came to hear him, even the kings of other countries.

At last Solomon began to build the great temple in Jerusalem which his father, David, had wished for. Solomon spared no effort or cost. It took seven years to build the temple, and it was very beautiful.

The house of the Lord was built of stone. The stone was fully cut before it was brought to the temple, so that no sound of a hammer or any tool was heard in that house.

And Solomon covered the temple with gold. And inside the Sanctuary there were statues of angels, each fifteen feet high. They were carved in olivewood and overlaid with gold.

When the Ark of the Covenant was brought into the temple, the glory of the Lord filled His house.

I KINGS

THE STORY OF JOB

Long after the reign of Solomon, the people of Israel were scattered far and wide in many lands. In the land of Uz there was a man named Job, who loved God with all his heart and with all his soul. Every morning he rose before dawn to give thanks to God and to sing His praise. All through the day Job remembered God and was glad.

Job was blessed by God and came to own vast herds of sheep and cattle. He had many children, who grew up and became owners of their own houses.

When Job's children were grown, there came a day when Satan talked with God in heaven. Satan was a creature capable of terrible evil.

Satan said to God, "I have been going to and fro, up and down all over the world, looking for a truly good man."

And God answered, "Have you found Job? He is a good man."

Satan did not believe that any man was truly good. He said to God, "Job loves you because you have given him so much. If he were to lose everything he has, he would curse your name."

God believed in Job's love, so He let Satan put Job to a hard test.

First Satan killed all the oxen and sheep and camels that belonged to Job. Then he sent murderers to kill Job's servants. Finally he sent a whirlwind that destroyed the house where Job's sons and daughters were gathered, and his children were killed.

When Job learned of all these things, he wept and fell on the ground. But he did not turn from God. "The Lord gives and the Lord takes away," he said. "Blessed be the name of the Lord."

Satan was very angry when he saw that Job still loved God. He had promised that he would spare Job's life, but Satan sent a horrible disease that invaded Job's body and covered it with sores.

Job was ill and in pain, and no sleep came to him in the night. His suffering was almost more than he could bear. At last Job cried out to God. "If I have sinned," he called to Him, "how did I injure Thee?"

But God knew that Job could not understand the ways of the Lord. Neither could he understand creation, when the first light appeared, or when Adam first drew breath, or the morning stars when they sang, or the way the hawk could soar or the eagle mount to the sky.

God spoke to Job of these things.

"The world of God is too wonderful for me to know," said Job, and he was sorry that he had doubted God.

And God healed Job and brought his children and his servants and all his animals back to him, and Job marveled at the greatness of the Lord.

JOB

THE FIERY FURNACE

When the Israelites had been driven out of their homeland, some of them lived in a place known as Babylon.

Nebuchadnezzar, the king of Babylon, built a tall image made of gold and demanded that everyone kneel down and worship the statue. All the people did as Nebuchadnezzar commanded, all except three men of Israel named Shadrach, Meshach, and Abednego. These men prayed only to the God of their fathers and would kneel before no other god.

In a rage the king said to the three, "If you do not pray to the golden image, I will have you thrown into a fiery furnace!"

The three men said to the king, "We can pray only to the God of gods. If you throw us in the fire, He will protect us."

Nebuchadnezzar was in a fury. He ordered the men to be thrown into a furnace that was fiery hot.

The king watched and waited for the men to fall down and die in the fire. But Shadrach, Meshach, and Abednego walked in the midst of the fire and were not burned. And the king saw a fourth person with them who was an angel of the Lord.

The king brought the men out of the fire and saw that they had not been touched by it. "These men put their trust in their God, and He has saved them," said the king. "Blessed be the God of Shadrach, Meshach, and Abednego."

DANIEL

Daniel in the Lions' Den

In Babylon in the days of King Darius, there lived an Israelite named Daniel. Daniel was a good man and also wise. King Darius knew this and gave Daniel great power. The other members of the court were jealous and wanted to destroy Daniel.

His enemies tricked the king into passing a new law. The law said that the people could not pray to anyone but the king for one month.

During that month, Daniel prayed as he always did to the God of his fathers, the God of Israel. When his enemies saw this, they told the king. "Daniel is not obeying your law," they said. "As punishment, he must be thrown to the lions. It is the law."

The king could do nothing and felt great sorrow.

"I cannot save you, Daniel," he said. "Pray to your God, that He may take care of you."

Daniel was led to the lions' den and thrown inside. The cave was sealed with a huge stone so that he could not escape.

That night the king could not sleep. Before dawn the next morning, he removed the stone from the lions' den and called into the dark cave, hoping that Daniel might still be alive.

"I am here, O King," Daniel answered. "I prayed, and God heard me. He sent an angel to close the mouths of the lions, and they did not harm me."

And the king brought Daniel out of the cave.

DANIEL

JONAH AND THE WHALE

In the land of the Assyrians, there lived a people who worshipped idols and did not love God. In that land, too, lived Jonah, a Hebrew, who was a good man and faithful to God.

God spoke to Jonah. "Go to the wicked city of Nineveh, in Assyria," He said. "Go now, and tell the people that they must change their ways."

Jonah did not want to go to Nineveh, so he went to a town by the sea and found a ship bound for a far-off land. Jonah hoped to travel so far that God could not find him.

While Jonah was on the ship, God made a hurricane at sea. The ship was tossed by mighty winds and waves, and the sailors were afraid. They prayed to their gods, but their gods did not answer them.

During the storm, Jonah slept in the hold of the ship. But the captain awakened him and begged him to pray to his God for help.

Jonah did not have to pray for guidance. "My God is the God of heaven who made both land and sea," said Jonah. "It is because of me that this storm has come. Take me and throw me overboard, and the sea will grow calm."

The sailors prayed to Jonah's God, and they asked Him to forgive them. Then they took Jonah and threw him overboard, and the sea grew calm. The sailors thanked the God of Jonah that the ship was safe once more.

Once in the sea,
Jonah cried out to God.
He thought he would surely drown.
He did not know that God wanted him to live.

And God sent a great fish, a fish as big as a whale, and the fish swallowed Jonah. Jonah was washed into the belly of the fish, and there he stayed for three days and three nights.

In the great fish, Jonah prayed to God, thanking God for not letting him drown. "I called to You in my distress," said Jonah, "and You answered me."

Then God brought the fish to shore and opened its huge mouth, and Jonah struggled up onto dry land.

Then God spoke to Jonah again. "Go to the city of Nineveh," He said. "Go now, and tell the people to change their ways."

This time Jonah obeyed and went to the city. God told him what to say to the people, and Jonah listened. When he spoke to the people, his words were so powerful that even the king of Nineveh was sorry for his wickedness. Jonah told the people to pray to God with all their might. And they did pray, and God forgave them.

JONAH

THUS SAYS THE LORD

"I said to the prisoners, 'Go free,'
and to those in darkness, 'Come out and be seen.'
They shall find pasture in the desert sands
and grazing on all the dunes.
They shall neither hunger nor thirst,
no scorching heat or sun shall hurt them;
for one who loves them shall lead them
and take them to water at bubbling springs."
Thus says the Lord.

ISAIAH